The Longevity Dilemma: Outliving Your Resources

Decoding Social Security and its role in retirement

Economic Instability: Federal Debt and Impact on Retirees

Guaranteed Income Solutions: Making Sense of Annuities

Risk Management in Retirement: Addressing Inflation, Market Crashes, and More

Asset VS Income: What Truly Matters in Retirement

Creating Certainty in Uncertain Times: Roll of Insurance and Estate Planning

Strategizing Against the Odds: Planning for a Sustainable Retirement

Hey There, What's This Crisis All About?

The retirement crisis facing the Baby Boomer generation is a subject that demands our attention. It isn't just any crisis—this one has been brewing for a while, and now it's reaching a critical point. So, let's peel back the layers and shed some light on this issue. The origins of this crisis can be traced back to a combination of factors, including changes in pension plans, longer life expectancy, and rising healthcare costs. As if that wasn't enough, stagnant wage growth and economic downturns fueled the fire. These defining features represent an intricate web of challenges that have created a perfect storm for retirees. With the traditional pension plans fading into obscurity, and Social Security facing its own set of challenges, the burden of funding retirement has shifted significantly onto individuals. The implications are far-reaching, extending beyond the realm of personal finance to impact broader societal and economic landscapes. The crisis isn't just a matter of numbers; it's about the potential ripple effects that could destabilize the foundations of our social fabric. This crisis presents us with a stark reality: the very generation that once redefined cultural and economic norms is now grappling with an uncertain future. It's a wake-up call for all generations to recognize the urgency of addressing this crisis before it spirals out of control

Why Should We Care? Spotlight on the Boomer Generation

The significance of the Boomer generation cannot be overstated, as it has defined cultural shifts and influenced economies for decades. As this colossal cohort approaches retirement age, the implications are profound. Not only will their exodus from the workforce impact labor markets and pension systems, but it also heralds a seismic shift in consumer spending patterns and healthcare demands. This demographic bulge has been pivotal in shaping everything from political landscapes to housing markets. With their impending retirement, the very structure of our society is set to undergo significant transformation.

So, why should we care? Consider this: Boomers are not merely a statistical anomaly; they are our parents, grandparents, and neighbors. Their welfare directly impacts our own, whether through inheritance, healthcare infrastructure, or simply the joy of witnessing our elders live fulfilling lives. Ignoring their retirement challenges would be akin to turning a blind eye to our collective future.

This generation's story is intertwined with the fabric of modern history. From the societal upheaval of the '60s to their economic triumphs in the '80s, Boomers have not just shaped their own destinies; they have left an indelible mark on global culture. This same influence will reverberate through their golden years, impacting everything from healthcare innovation to leisure industries. By understanding and addressing the specific needs and challenges Boomers face as they retire, we can better prepare for societal changes and ensure that this generation continues to thrive and contribute meaningfully.

Teaser Time: What's Next in 'The Longevity Dilemma'

In the next chapter, we will delve into a fascinating yet concerning topic—a dilemma that has been lurking beneath the surface of our collective consciousness: The Longevity Dilemma. Imagine this: thanks to advances in healthcare and lifestyle improvements, people are living longer than ever before. On the surface, this seems like a cause for celebration. After all, who wouldn't want a few extra years to enjoy life? But here's the catch: the financial implications of increased longevity are not as rosy as one might hope. As individuals and as a society, we need to seriously consider how we will support an aging population that is living longer than previous generations. This chapter will peel back the layers of this complex issue, exploring the financial challenges and uncertainties associated with longevity. We'll uncover how prolonged lifespans impact retirement planning and the sustainability of pension systems. From the individual level to broader economic implications, we'll navigate the intricate web of considerations that come into play when we talk about living longer and its financial repercussions. Stay tuned for an eye-opening discussion on 'The Longevity Dilemma'.

Hang on, Are We Living Too Long?

We've all heard the good news: people are living longer. Thanks to a combination of cultural and medical advancements, life expectancies have been steadily increasing over the years. While this extended longevity is undoubtedly a cause for celebration, it also raises some critical questions regarding retirement planning. As we hang on to life for more years than ever before, the traditional approach to saving for retirement may no longer suffice. The implications of longer lives, both culturally and economically, are profound. It's no longer just about reaching retirement age; it's about ensuring that our savings can support us through potentially decades of post-career life. This shift in life expectancy has forced a re-evaluation of what it means to be financially secure in retirement. With the increasing number of active and healthy seniors, the traditional concept of retirement is evolving, and so should our approach to retirement planning. Longer lives mean more time to enjoy the fruits of our labor, but it also means needing more resources to sustain this extended period of post-employment life. The impact is not just personal. On a broader scale, increased life expectancies affect social security systems, healthcare infrastructure, and overall economic stability. As such, addressing the implications of longer lives requires a holistic perspective that goes beyond individual financial planning. Indeed, reckoning with the reality of living longer involves confronting multifaceted challenges and opportunities. The societal conversation around longevity is evolving from reimagining retirement savings strategies to embracing new aging paradigms. In the coming chapters, we will delve deeper into the financial intricacies of this longevity revolution and explore innovative solutions for ensuring financial security in an era where we're not just retiring but thriving well into our golden years.

Oops! Did We Save Enough?

When it comes to planning for retirement, one of the biggest concerns is whether we have saved enough money to sustain us through our golden years. Many people are taken aback by this question, as they may have neglected their retirement savings or underestimated the true cost of living post-retirement.

It's not uncommon for individuals to shy away from confronting this reality, but it's a crucial step in securing financial stability. The harsh truth is that life expectancy is increasing, and so are the associated expenses. Did you consider all the unexpected expenditures that could come your way during retirement? Medical bills, long-term care costs, and inflation are just some potential financial burdens that could jeopardize your savings. The earlier we acknowledge these possibilities, the better equipped we are to face them head-on. It's never too late to take stock of our financial situation and make necessary adjustments. If you're concerned about falling short on savings, don't lose hope. There are various tactics and strategies available to help bolster your retirement fund. Whether it's maximizing contributions to your employer-sponsored retirement plan or exploring additional investment opportunities, there are avenues to improve your financial standing. Seeking professional guidance to assess your current savings and develop a comprehensive plan can also yield valuable insights. Remember, it's okay to seek help and admit that you may not have everything figured out. The key is to remain proactive and open-minded in addressing these concerns. Let's face it — many of us wish we had saved more aggressively earlier on, but dwelling on the past won't change the present reality. Instead, channel your energy into taking positive steps towards securing your financial future. Owning up to our financial oversights can be a tough pill to swallow, but it's the first step toward rectifying our situation. Ultimately, the goal is not to dwell on regret but rather to proactively shape our financial destiny. By acknowledging any saving deficiencies, we pave the way for an informed, intentional approach to securing a comfortable retirement.

Life Expectancy Considerations

As we plan for our retirement, it becomes imperative to consider the aspect of life expectancy. With advancements in healthcare and technology, individuals are living longer lives today than ever before. This demographic shift directly impacts retirement planning as it necessitates a comprehensive understanding of potential longevity and its financial ramifications.

When contemplating life expectancy, it is essential to recognize that increased longevity also means an extended period of relying on retirement savings and potentially greater healthcare expenses. Therefore, it is crucial to incorporate life expectancy considerations into retirement planning to ensure that financial resources remain sustainable over the long term.

The process of assessing life expectancy involves considering various factors such as family medical history, current health status, lifestyle choices, and broader societal trends in life expectancy. Leveraging this information allows for a more accurate estimation of how long retirement savings need to last and what level of healthcare expenditures may be incurred.

Moreover, the evolution of life expectancy projections underscores the need for flexibility in retirement planning. While individuals may have traditionally anticipated retiring at a specific age, the possibility of living longer necessitates reassessing retirement timelines and income strategies. This adaptability ensures that financial plans align with the reality of increased life expectancies.

In addition to financial considerations, contemplating life expectancy enables individuals to make informed decisions regarding legacy planning and potential care needs in later stages of life. By acknowledging the prospect of an extended lifespan, retirees can proactively address these aspects, thereby providing peace of mind for themselves and their loved ones.

Ultimately, integrating life expectancy considerations into retirement planning empowers individuals to cultivate a holistic and resilient approach to securing their financial future. By recognizing and accounting for the potential length of retirement and associated financial obligations, individuals can develop comprehensive strategies that mitigate the risks of outliving their assets and provide a sense of stability throughout their retirement years.

Assessing Your Risk Tolerance

Investing for retirement entails navigating through different levels of risk. Understanding and assessing your risk tolerance is a critical aspect of developing a sound retirement strategy. Risk tolerance refers to your willingness and ability to endure fluctuations in the value of your investments in pursuit of potentially higher returns. As you plan for retirement, it's essential to evaluate your comfort level with market fluctuations and potential investment losses. To assess your risk tolerance, consider various factors such as your investment goals, time horizon, financial situation, and emotional temperament. Your investment goals should align with your risk tolerance. If your goal is long-term wealth accumulation, you might have a greater capacity to take on more aggressive, growth-oriented investments. On the other hand, if your primary goal is capital preservation for near-term retirement, you may opt for more conservative and income-generating investments. Your time horizon plays a vital role in determining your risk tolerance. Longer time horizons allow for a greater ability to tolerate short-term market fluctuations, making long-term investments potentially more suitable. Conversely, minimizing exposure to high-risk assets could be a priority if you're nearing retirement. Your current financial situation and liquidity needs also influence your risk tolerance. Evaluating your cash flow requirements and emergency funds can help determine the level of risk you can comfortably assume. Regularly reassessing your risk tolerance can ensure that your retirement strategy remains in sync with your evolving financial goals and personal comfort levels.

Planning for the Future: Roth Conversions

One key strategy that often goes overlooked is the concept of Roth conversions. This powerful financial tool can help you optimize your retirement savings and create a tax-efficient plan for the future. Imagine this: You've diligently saved money in traditional retirement accounts over the years, enjoying the tax-deferred growth and contributions. But as you approach retirement, you start thinking about the taxes you'll owe when you start withdrawing that money. This is where Roth conversions come into play. Roth conversions allow you to transfer funds from a traditional IRA or 401(k) into a Roth IRA. By doing this, you can potentially reduce your future tax burden, as qualified distributions from a Roth IRA are tax-free. This can be especially beneficial if you anticipate being in a higher tax bracket in retirement.

But here's the catch: when you convert funds from a traditional account to a Roth IRA, you'll have to pay taxes on the converted amount in the year of the conversion. This may seem daunting at first, but the long-term tax benefits can outweigh the short-term tax hit. When planning for Roth conversions, it's important to consider your current tax situation, your anticipated retirement income, and your long-term financial goals. By working with a retirement specialist and tax professional, you can create a customized conversion strategy that maximizes the tax advantages while minimizing any potential drawbacks. Roth conversions can offer several benefits beyond tax efficiency. For example, unlike traditional IRAs, Roth IRAs do not have required minimum distributions (RMDs) once you reach age 73. This can give you more flexibility in managing your retirement income and tax situation, allowing you to leave a legacy for your heirs if you wish.

Additionally, Roth conversions can serve as a valuable estate planning tool. By paying taxes on the converted amount now, you can effectively "prepay" the tax liability on those assets, potentially reducing the size of your taxable estate and maximizing the amount you can pass on to your beneficiaries tax-free. While Roth conversions can be a powerful strategy, they are not without considerations and potential drawbacks. For example, if you expect your tax rate to be lower in retirement or if you do not have enough cash on hand to pay the taxes due on the conversion, a Roth conversion may not be the best choice for you.

Roth conversions can be a valuable tool for building a tax-efficient retirement plan that provides you with flexibility, control, and peace of mind in your golden years. By carefully evaluating your financial situation, goals, and tax implications and working with a tax professional, you can make informed decisions that set you up for a secure and prosperous future. It is crucial to note that the tax implications of Roth conversions can vary based on individual circumstances. Factors such as future tax brackets, retirement income sources, and potential tax law changes should all be carefully considered before executing a Roth conversion strategy. Another important aspect to consider is the timing of Roth conversions. Converting funds during years when your income is lower or when tax rates are favorable can maximize the tax benefits of the conversion. Additionally, spreading out conversions over multiple years can help mitigate the tax impact and allow for better planning of cash flow needs. Furthermore, it's essential to understand the rules surrounding Roth Conversions and consult a tax professional. When considering Roth conversions, reviewing your overall retirement plan holistically is essential. Taking into account other sources of income, such as Social Security benefits, pensions, and investment accounts, can help you determine the optimal strategy for incorporating Roth conversions into your retirement income plan. By strategically integrating Roth conversions, you can reduce your overall tax liability in retirement and enhance the longevity of your retirement savings. In the ever-changing landscape of retirement planning, Roth conversions offer a flexible and tax-efficient way to optimize your retirement savings and create a legacy for future generations. By working with a tax professional and carefully evaluating your individual circumstances, you can make informed decisions that align with your financial goals and set you on the path to a secure and comfortable retirement.

Understanding Social Security: Basics and Importance

Social Security is a federal program designed to provide financial support to individuals who have retired or are disabled, as well as to the survivors of deceased workers. It emerged in response to the economic challenges faced by aging populations and has played a pivotal role in alleviating poverty among retirees. The program operates on the principle of social insurance, where current workers contribute a portion of their earnings to support current beneficiaries, with the expectation of receiving similar benefits when they retire. This intergenerational funding model underpins the stability and long-term sustainability of Social Security. One of the key components of Social Security is retirement benefits, which serve as a foundation for many Americans' post-work life. These benefits are aimed at replacing a portion of an individual's pre-retirement income, ensuring a degree of financial security during their later years. Additionally, Social Security provides disability benefits to individuals who are unable to work due to a qualifying medical condition. By providing this safety net, Social Security helps preserve the financial well-being of these vulnerable individuals. Another critical aspect of Social Security is its survivor benefits, which offer crucial financial assistance to the dependents of deceased workers. This support can be especially vital for families facing the sudden loss of a breadwinner. Overall, the significance of Social Security cannot be overstated. It serves as a cornerstone of retirement planning for millions of Americans, offering financial stability and peace of mind during their golden years.

The History of Social Security and Its Evolution

Social Security, established in 1935 under President Franklin D. Roosevelt's administration, was a landmark program designed to provide financial security for retired workers. The historical context of its development is essential for understanding its significance today. At the time of its inception, the United States was grappling with the widespread economic turmoil of the Great Depression. Millions of Americans were left destitute, and there was an urgent need for social welfare programs to prevent further societal disintegration. Recognizing this imperative, President Roosevelt and the Congress worked diligently to create a safety net that would prevent seniors from falling into poverty during their retirement years. The original Social Security Act aimed at addressing not only the issue of poverty among the elderly but also unemployment insurance, aid to dependent children, and grants to states for various public health services. This comprehensive approach underscored the government's commitment to safeguarding the well-being of its citizens. Over the decades, Social Security has evolved in response to demographic shifts, economic changes, and political developments. Amendments and reforms have been instituted to ensure its sustainability while adapting to the evolving needs of retirees. The program's expansion to include disability benefits and survivor benefits illustrates its responsiveness to the changing nature of social and economic challenges. Moreover, amendments in the 1980s and 1990s sought to address financial issues, leading to adjustments in taxation and benefit calculations. Understanding this historical evolution provides crucial insights into the systemic intricacies of Social Security and underscores its status as a cornerstone of the U.S. social welfare system. By examining the historical progression of Social Security, we gain a deeper appreciation of its pivotal role in shaping retirement planning and the broader socio-economic landscape.

Eligibility Criteria for Social Security Benefits

To ensure a financially secure retirement, understanding the eligibility criteria for Social Security benefits is paramount. Eligibility is primarily determined by an individual's work history and contributions to the Social Security system. As per the guidelines set forth by the Social Security Administration (SSA), individuals become eligible for retirement benefits once they have earned a specified number of credits through working in jobs covered by Social Security. These credits are earned based on annual income and are used to determine eligibility for various Social Security programs. For most individuals, achieving the required 40 credits or roughly 10 years of work is sufficient to qualify for retirement benefits. Additionally, survivors and disability benefits have their own unique eligibility criteria, often requiring a different number of credits depending on the specific circumstances. It's important to note that the eligibility requirements can change over time as policies and regulations are updated. Therefore, it is crucial to stay informed about these changes to ensure that one meets the necessary criteria when planning for retirement. While the basic eligibility criteria provide a general framework, it's essential to consider individual circumstances, such as marital status, dependent children, and specific medical conditions, which may affect eligibility for certain types of benefits. Engaging with a retirement strategist or leveraging online resources provided by the SSA can offer valuable insight into the intricacies of eligibility criteria and how they apply to personal retirement planning. By being well-informed about eligibility requirements, individuals can make strategic decisions when it comes to incorporating Social Security benefits into their overall retirement strategy, enhancing their financial security in the long term.

How Benefits Are Calculated

When considering retirement and the role of Social Security benefits, understanding how these benefits are calculated is crucial. The primary factor in determining your Social Security benefit amount is your earnings history. The Social Security Administration (SSA) tracks your income over your working years and calculates your Average Indexed Monthly Earnings (AIME). This figure forms the basis for determining your primary insurance amount (PIA), which is the amount you are eligible to receive at full retirement age. To arrive at this PIA, a formula is applied that takes into account specific percentages of your AIME up to a certain threshold known as the 'bend points.' Understanding these bend points and how they affect benefit calculations is essential for individuals planning their retirement finances. It's worth noting that your actual benefit can vary depending on when you choose to start receiving payments. Claiming benefits before full retirement age will result in proportional reductions, while delaying claims beyond full retirement age can lead to increased benefits due to delayed retirement credits. Additionally, spouses may also be entitled to benefits based on their partner's work history, adding another layer of complexity to benefit calculations. The intricate nature of these calculations underscores the need for careful consideration and financial planning when deciding on the optimal time to commence receiving Social Security benefits. By gaining a comprehensive understanding of how benefits are calculated and taking into account individual circumstances, retirees can maximize their Social Security payouts and enhance their overall financial security in retirement.

Timing Your Social Security Claims for Maximum Benefit

When it comes to Social Security benefits, timing is crucial. The age at which you choose to start receiving benefits can significantly impact the amount you receive over your retirement years. Understanding the optimal timing for claiming your Social Security benefits is essential for maximizing your income and ensuring long-term financial security. Several key factors should be considered when determining the ideal time to initiate your claims. Firstly, the earliest age at which you can claim Social Security benefits is 62, but doing so will result in reduced monthly payments. On the other hand, delaying your benefits beyond your full retirement age (typically between 66 and 67, depending on the year of birth) can lead to increased monthly payouts through delayed retirement credits. By waiting until age 70, individuals can maximize their benefits by accruing the highest possible monthly amount. However, the decision to delay claiming benefits must be weighed against individual circumstances, such as health, life expectancy, and current financial needs. Furthermore, factoring in spousal or survivor benefits adds complexity to the timing decision. For married couples, considering strategies that optimize both spouses' benefits is crucial to maximize their joint income throughout retirement. Implementing a coordinated approach to timing benefit claims can facilitate the achievement of maximum combined benefits. It's essential to recognize that the decision regarding Social Security claim timing is highly personalized and should align with your overall retirement plan. Consulting with a financial advisor or retirement strategist utilizing specialized software to model various claiming scenarios based on your personal circumstances can provide valuable insights. By carefully evaluating these considerations and planning strategically, you can optimize your Social Security benefits and enhance your financial well-being in retirement.

Tax Implications of Social Security Benefits

Social Security benefits can be a crucial source of income during retirement, but it is important to understand the tax implications associated with these benefits. Many retirees are surprised by the impact taxes can have on their Social Security income. The taxation of Social Security benefits depends on the recipient's provisional income, which includes half of the Social Security benefits, all taxable income, and certain tax-exempt interest. Understanding the taxation thresholds is essential for effective retirement income planning. Individuals with a higher provisional income may be subject to income tax on a larger portion of their Social Security benefits. It's important to note that up to 85% of Social Security benefits may be subject to income tax for individuals with higher provisional incomes. This underscores the need for careful tax planning and asset allocation strategies in retirement. Retirees should consider various tactics to minimize the impact of taxes on their Social Security benefits. These may include managing withdrawals from tax-deferred retirement accounts, such as IRAs and 401(k)s, to control provisional income. Additionally, investing in tax-efficient vehicles and maximizing contributions to tax-advantaged accounts can help mitigate the tax burden on Social Security income. Proper tax planning also involves understanding how other sources of retirement income, such as pensions, annuities, and investment dividends, may affect the taxation of Social Security benefits. The complexity of tax implications underscores the importance of seeking professional advice, such as consulting with a retirement strategist and tax advisor, to develop a comprehensive tax strategy tailored to individual retirement goals. Lastly, staying informed about changes in tax laws and regulations, as well as periodic reviews of one's tax strategy, is paramount for optimizing the tax efficiency of one's retirement income. By being proactive and informed about the tax implications of Social Security benefits, retirees can better position themselves to maximize their overall retirement income while minimizing unnecessary tax liabilities.

Common Pitfalls and How to Avoid Them

Navigating the complexities of Social Security benefits can be rife with potential pitfalls that individuals approaching retirement should be aware of. One common pitfall is failing to understand the implications of additional income on Social Security benefits. As an individual continues to work while receiving Social Security, certain benefits may be subject to taxation if their combined income exceeds a certain threshold. This lack of awareness could lead to unexpected tax burdens and financial strain. Another pitfall is claiming benefits too early out of necessity without considering the long-term impact. While it may seem beneficial to start receiving benefits as soon as possible, doing so could result in significantly reduced monthly payments over the course of retirement. Moreover, individuals who haven't reached full retirement age might experience penalties for earning above a certain limit if they claim benefits prematurely. Furthermore, not factoring in the impact of health and life expectancy can also pose risks. Some individuals may underestimate their life expectancy and fail to maximize their benefits, while others may overestimate it, leading to suboptimal claiming decisions. Failing to coordinate spousal benefits effectively is another potential pitfall. Couples should carefully strategize to ensure they make the most of combined benefits. Additionally, overlooking survivor benefits can be a costly mistake. With careful planning, individuals can avoid these common pitfalls. Engaging early with retirement planners and a tax professional who understands retirement strategies, not just taxes, is crucial for making informed decisions about Social Security. Financial literacy and proactive research play pivotal roles in avoiding missteps. It's imperative for individuals to stay informed about any legislative changes affecting Social Security and periodically reassess their claiming strategy to adapt to evolving regulations.

Future of Social Security: Trends and Predictions

The future of Social Security is a topic of great interest and concern for current and future retirees. As the population demographics shift with an increasing number of retirees and a smaller proportion of working individuals, the sustainability of the Social Security system has come into question. Several trends and predictions have emerged that shed light on what the future may hold for this crucial retirement benefit. One significant trend is the projected depletion of the Social Security trust fund. According to the Trustees of the Social Security Administration, the trust fund reserves are expected to be exhausted by 2034 if no corrective actions are taken. This has raised concerns about the potential reduction in benefits that future retirees may receive. Another important trend is the changing societal dynamics, including longer life expectancies and shifting employment patterns. These factors are placing additional strain on the Social Security system as more individuals are drawing benefits for extended periods. As a result, policymakers are exploring various proposals to address these challenges and ensure the long-term viability of Social Security. Among the potential solutions being debated are adjustments to the retirement age, changes to benefit calculations, and potential increases in payroll taxes. Additionally, there is growing discussion about the role of private savings and investments in supplementing Social Security benefits. Some experts predict a shift towards greater reliance on personal retirement accounts and employer-sponsored plans to complement Social Security income. This would require individuals to take greater responsibility for their own retirement planning and financial security. Furthermore, advancements in technology and data analytics are expected to play a key role in shaping the future administration of Social Security. The use of digital platforms and automation may streamline processes and improve the efficiency of benefit disbursement while enhancing fraud prevention measures. Overall, the future of Social Security presents both challenges and opportunities. It calls for thoughtful consideration, proactive planning, and informed decision-making to adapt to the evolving landscape of retirement benefits and ensure financial stability for future generations.

Riding the Roller Coaster: Understanding Federal Debt

The history of federal debt is akin to a roller coaster ride through the peaks and valleys of economic progress. A journey that commenced with the birth of the nation, where debt was incurred to finance wars and stabilize the economy. Following periods of debt reduction and stability, the Great Depression and World War II ushered in significant spikes in federal borrowing. Post-war economic prosperity briefly tempered debt levels before entering a new era of growth spurred by social programs and military expenditure. The 1980s witnessed a drastic surge in federal debt, attributed to tax cuts and increased defense spending. This trend continued into subsequent decades, punctuated by intermittent efforts at fiscal prudence. Fast forward to the present day, and we find ourselves grappling with unprecedented levels of national debt resulting from various economic factors and political decisions. Each crest and trough of this financial roller coaster has left an indelible mark on the economic landscape, impacting citizens across generations.

How Retirees Feel the Pinch: The Real World Impact

Federal debt can have a very real impact on retirees, influencing everything from the stability of Social Security to the overall health of the economy. As the national debt grows, retirees may start to feel the pinch in various ways. One major concern is that an increasing federal debt could lead to higher interest rates and inflation. This, in turn, could erode the purchasing power of retirees' fixed incomes, making it harder for them to cover everyday living expenses. Moreover, a ballooning federal debt could also strain the government's ability to fund entitlement programs, such as Social Security and Medicare. Retirees who depend on these benefits for a significant portion of their income could face uncertainty and potential benefit cuts. Furthermore, high federal debt levels can create economic instability, leading to market volatility, reduced investment returns, and a generally less favorable environment for savings and retirement portfolios. This can directly impact retirees' financial security and ability to sustain their desired lifestyles in retirement. In addition, federal debt has implications for future generations. As the burden of paying down this debt falls on younger taxpayers, the resources available for supporting retirees through social programs and healthcare may become increasingly strained. This can have intergenerational impacts that affect retirees' families and descendants. On a broader level, federal debt also threatens the overall strength and stability of the U.S. economy, which can impact retirees in numerous ways. For instance, a weaker economy might result in fewer job opportunities for retirees seeking part-time work to supplement their income or relaunch their careers. It may also impact the value of investments and pension funds, affecting retirees' long-term financial plans. These are just a few examples of how federal debt can significantly impact retirees in the real world. Addressing these challenges requires a multifaceted approach that considers current retiree needs and the future sustainability of economic and social systems.

Bridging the Gap: Strategies to Weather Economic Storms

In times of economic instability and mounting federal debt, retirees often find themselves facing unparalleled challenges. The impact on their financial security can be profound, as market volatility and uncertain fiscal policies create a wave of uncertainty. To weather these storms, retirees must adopt strategies that offer resilience and stability. One such strategy is diversification. By spreading investments across different asset classes, retirees can mitigate the impact of market downturns on their overall portfolio. Additionally, maintaining a healthy cash reserve can provide a buffer against unexpected expenses or market corrections. Another crucial aspect of bridging the economic gap is prudent budgeting and expense management. Retirees must carefully assess their spending habits and prioritize essential costs while seeking ways to trim unnecessary expenditures. This not only helps in managing day-to-day finances but also ensures that retirees have sufficient funds to withstand economic turbulence. Moreover, evaluating and adjusting one's risk tolerance as retirement progresses is vital. A conservative approach might be more appropriate in the face of economic uncertainties, ensuring that investments align with shifting financial needs. Furthermore, considering guaranteed income solutions, such as annuities, can provide a reliable income stream irrespective of market fluctuations. This shields retirees from the impact of economic downturns and aids in fulfilling ongoing financial requirements. Finally, seeking professional guidance from retirement specialists can offer valuable insights and tailored strategies to navigate through economic upheavals. With their expertise, retirees can chart a course that addresses their unique circumstances and aligns with their long-term financial goals. By implementing these proactive measures, retirees can better insulate themselves from the adverse effects of economic instability and federal debt.

Decoding Annuities: What Are They Really?

An annuity is like a special account you set up with an insurance company that grows on a tax-deferred basis. It's the only financial product of its kind that is designed to provide a guaranteed income stream for life or a set period, starting either immediately or in the future. Essentially, it's a long-term contract between you and the insurance company. Think of it as laying the groundwork for a stable source of income during retirement, ensuring you won't outlive your savings. This can offer peace of mind, knowing that no matter what happens in the market or how long you live, you'll continue receiving payments as agreed upon. Annuities also provide a valuable opportunity to grow your retirement assets with the potential of an ongoing income stream. Understanding the basic concept and function of annuities in a retirement plan is fundamental to effectively utilize them to secure your financial future.

Types of Annuities: One Size Does Not Fit All

When it comes to annuities, one size certainly does not fit all. There are various types of annuities, each designed to serve different purposes and suit different financial needs. Understanding the differences between these types is crucial in making informed decisions about your retirement income. Let's dive into the diverse landscape of annuities to unpack their individual features and benefits.

Fixed Annuities: This type of annuity offers a guaranteed payout at regular intervals. With fixed annuities, you have the assurance of a steady stream of income, providing stability and predictability. It's an appealing option for those seeking a secure foundation for their retirement income, as the risk is assumed by the insurance company rather than the annuitant. However, it's important to weigh the potential drawbacks, such as limited growth potential due to fixed interest rates.

Variable Annuities: Unlike fixed annuities, variable annuities offer the opportunity for growth through investment in sub-accounts that resemble mutual funds. This means that the returns from variable annuities are tied to the performance of the underlying investments, presenting the possibility of higher returns but also carrying greater risk.

Immediate Annuities: As the name suggests, immediate annuities start providing payouts soon after a lump sum is invested. They are ideal for individuals who require an immediate and predictable source of income following retirement or as part of their overall financial plan. Immediate annuities offer the security of a guaranteed income stream, allowing retirees to cover essential expenses without ongoing market risks.

Deferred Annuities: In contrast to immediate annuities, deferred annuities begin their payout phase at a future date specified by the annuitant. This type of annuity enables individuals to accumulate tax-deferred savings over time, often during their working years, and defer payouts until retirement when they may be in a lower tax bracket. By deferring the commencement of payments, annuitants can grow their assets through investments until they're ready to receive regular income.

Fixed Index Annuities: Combining elements of both fixed and variable annuities, fixed index annuities offer the potential for interest credits based on the performance of a market index, while ensuring a minimum guaranteed interest rate. This hybrid structure provides a balance of growth potential and downside protection, making it a compelling choice for those seeking market-linked returns without exposing their principal to market downturns.

Understanding the distinctions among these annuity types is pivotal in aligning your retirement income strategy with your specific financial objectives and risk tolerance. Each type presents unique advantages and considerations, emphasizing the need for thorough evaluation and professional guidance. Every annuity works a specific way. Working with an annuity specialist that will compare which one is right for you is crucial. There is no one-size-fits-all in the annuity world. Also, stacking annuities to offer you different payout options can maximize your retirement portfolio. Did you know that annuities bypass probate and are creditor-protected? With this understanding, you'll be better equipped to navigate the array of annuity options with your retirement specialist and tailor your choices to your retirement aspirations.

Calculating the Cash: How Annuities Pay Out

Annuities come with different payout options, and understanding how these payments work is crucial in making informed decisions for your retirement strategy. The calculation of annuity payouts can vary based on several factors, including the type of annuity you choose – whether it's a fixed, variable, or indexed annuity. Each type comes with its unique payout structure that influences how your cash flows. Fixed annuities offer a predetermined payout based on the agreed-upon interest rate, providing a level of stability. On the other hand, variable annuities tie payouts to the performance of the underlying investments, offering potential for higher returns but also exposing you to market risks. Indexed annuities provide a middle ground, linking payouts to specific market indexes, offering a balance between stability and growth potential. Many offer lifetime incomes, as well as long term care type benefits. Another critical factor in calculating annuity payouts is the age at which you start receiving them. Generally, the older you are when you begin receiving payouts, the higher the amount you'll receive. This is because annuity providers factor in life expectancy, so starting payouts at an older age means they expect to make fewer payments, thus offering you a larger sum per payment. Moreover, the frequency of payments also impacts the overall payout structure. Whether you opt for monthly, quarterly, or annual payments will influence the total amount you'll receive over time. Additionally, some annuities offer beneficiaries the option to continue receiving payments after the annuitant's passing, ensuring that loved ones benefit from the investment. It's important to consider all these variables and intricacies when evaluating annuity payout options to ensure they align with your financial goals and circumstances. Overall, understanding the mechanics behind how annuities pay out empowers you to choose the most suitable option for securing a reliable income stream during retirement.

Battling the Invisible Thief: Guarding Against Inflation

Inflation, often called the 'invisible thief,' has the power to silently erode the purchasing power of retirement savings. As prices rise over time, a fixed income can struggle to cover everyday expenses, leaving retirees vulnerable. Addressing inflation becomes a critical component of retirement planning. Fortunately, several strategies exist to shield savings from the effects of inflation.

Another pivotal strategy involves incorporating an adaptable withdrawal plan that accounts for inflation. By adjusting withdrawals to align with the increasing cost of living, retirees can strive to preserve their standard of living throughout retirement. Furthermore, exploring annuities can provide a reliable source of income that adjusts for inflation, offering a safeguard against the impact of rising prices.

Moreover, maintaining a proactive stance towards healthcare planning is crucial in combating the erosion caused by inflation. Healthcare expenses tend to surge with age, and overlooking this component can lead to financial strain. Therefore, strategic health and long-term care insurance coverage can fortify safeguards against the escalating costs associated with aging.

Weathering the Storm: Surviving and Thriving During Market Crashes

Imagine waking up one morning, turning on the news, and finding out that the stock market has plummeted overnight, AGAIN. The panic sets in as you watch your hard-earned savings seemingly evaporate before your eyes. Market crashes can be terrifying, but they don't have to be catastrophic if you're prepared. In this section, we'll delve into strategies for weathering the storm, not just surviving but thriving during market crashes. First and foremost, it's vital to maintain a long-term perspective. Market downturns are a natural part of the economic cycle, and historically, markets have always recovered from crashes. By sticking to a well-thought-out investment plan and not giving in to fear-based decisions, you stand a greater chance of emerging unscathed. Diversification also plays a crucial role in mitigating the impact of market crashes. Spreading your investments across different asset classes can help cushion the blow when one sector takes a hit. Furthermore, having a cash reserve for emergencies can provide comfort and stability during turbulent times. It's often said that the best time to prepare for a market crash is before it happens. Building a resilient portfolio through careful asset allocation and risk management is key to weathering the storm with confidence. Aside from diversifying and maintaining a long-term view, staying informed and seeking professional advice can significantly bolster your ability to navigate market crashes effectively. Monitoring economic indicators, understanding market dynamics, and speaking with financial experts can provide valuable insights and guidance during tumultuous times. Additionally, Annuities and Life insurance products designed to protect against market volatility can offer an extra layer of security. Market crashes are an unavoidable aspect of investing, but they don't have to derail your financial future. By adopting a strategic approach, keeping a level head, and taking proactive measures, you can not only survive market crashes but also position yourself to thrive in the aftermath. Establishing a guaranteed income stream is first and foremost in successful retirement planning.

The Miscellaneous Minefield: Navigating Other Financial Risks

Now that we've explored the tumultuous terrain of market crashes, it's time to shine a spotlight on the other lurking hazards that could threaten your financial well-being in retirement. These lesser-known dangers may not make the headlines like stock market plunges do, but they still have the potential to wreak havoc on your hard-earned nest egg. Let's start by delving into the intricate web of tax risks. As your retirement income streams flow from various sources, you will need to be wary of how taxes can take a hefty bite out of your funds. Make sure you have a forward-thinking CPA or Tax Professional who will work together with your Retirement Planner to properly help you understand the tax implications of your investment decisions. It can make a significant difference in preserving your wealth. Next, let's venture into the realm of healthcare costs, an often-underestimated peril that can ambush retirees. With medical expenses on the rise, it's crucial to have a robust strategy in place to cushion the impact of potential health-related financial burdens. Long-term care insurance and health savings accounts are just some of the tools that can safeguard you against this threat. Another minefield to navigate is the possibility of longevity risk, which refers to the chance of outliving your retirement savings. As we continue to enjoy longer lifespans, this risk becomes increasingly pertinent. Crafting a sustainable withdrawal plan and exploring annuities or other longevity protection products can serve as valuable shields against this hazard. Lastly, we must also acknowledge the danger posed by unexpected events such as home repairs, car replacements, and other unplanned expenditures. While these may seem minor in isolation, they can add up to a substantial drain on your resources if not accounted for. By building an emergency fund and incorporating these potential costs into your retirement budget, you can fortify your financial fortress against these miscellaneous perils. Remember, while market crashes are attention-grabbing, managing these lesser-known financial risks is equally essential in ensuring a secure and stress-free retirement journey.

Nest Egg or Cash Flow? Setting the Stage

As we embark on the retirement planning journey, a crucial consideration emerges: the balance between having a substantial 'nest egg' and securing consistent income to meet day-to-day expenses. The concept of a 'nest egg' often conjures images of a hefty sum in a savings account or investment portfolio, providing a safety net for the future. While this backbone is undeniably important, it's equally vital to ensure that this accumulation can translate into sustainable cash flow throughout retirement. Achieving the delicate equilibrium between an abundant nest egg and reliable cash flow is central to attaining financial security and peace of mind during our golden years.

To confront the dichotomy between a sizeable nest egg and dependable cash flow, we must first appreciate their distinct roles. The 'nest egg' represents the pool of assets amassed over one's working years, encompassing 401(k) funds, IRAs, stocks, bonds, and other investments. These reserves serve as a reservoir from which to draw upon for future needs, offering a cushion against unforeseen expenses, healthcare costs, and lifestyle aspirations. On the other hand, regular income – often derived from Social Security benefits, pensions, annuities, and other sources – forms the bedrock of day-to-day financial sustenance. Striking a harmonious chord between these two dynamics demands dexterity in navigating the intricacies of investment strategies, social security claiming tactics, and other financial vehicles.

Yet, the quest for balance extends beyond mere monetary considerations. It delves into the realm of emotional well-being, transcending the numbers to encapsulate the essence of enjoying retired life without fretting about finances. Reconciling the allure of a sizeable nest egg with the imperative of steady cash flow beckons us to ponder profound questions about our post-retirement ambitions, risk tolerance, and overall financial objectives. Do we prioritize travel and experiences, requiring a more robust cash flow, or are we content with a modest lifestyle, placing greater emphasis on the nest egg's magnitude? These deliberations underscore the deeply personal nature of retirement planning and the need to tailor financial plans to align with individual dreams and aspirations. This juncture illuminates the holistic nature of retirement preparedness, where the interplay between asset accumulation and distribution unfolds against the backdrop of individual preferences and broader life goals. There are three phases of Retirement: Accumulation, Distribution, and Preservation. Having a Retirement Professional that understands these phases and works with you to build a strategic retirement plan is crucial in a successful, happy retirement.

Decoding What Pays the Bills: Assets vs. Income Breakdown

When it comes to planning for retirement, there's a constant debate about whether it's more important to focus on building up a substantial nest egg or establishing reliable cash flow for the future. This debate essentially boils down to the distinction between assets and income. Let's break it down. Assets refer to what you own – your investments, property, and savings. Meanwhile, income is the money that flows into your accounts regularly, such as through pensions, annuities, or social security. Understanding the difference between these two is crucial to ensuring financial stability in retirement. Many retirees make the mistake of fixating solely on their assets, believing that a large sum of money stored away will guarantee a comfortable retirement. While having a healthy nest egg is undeniably important, it's equally critical to consider how you'll generate income from those assets once you're no longer working. This brings us to the pivotal concept of cash flow - the lifeblood of retirement. You can possess significant assets, but if they aren't generating a consistent stream of income, they may not effectively support your lifestyle in retirement. On the other hand, prioritizing income alone without considering the growth and sustainability of your assets could also lead to potential financial instability down the road. So, it's not an 'either/or' situation, but rather a careful balance between the two. Understanding this interplay is essential for decoding what really pays the bills in retirement. As we delve into the intricacies of asset allocation, investment diversity, and creating passive income streams, we'll gain a clearer vision of how both assets and income are instrumental in ensuring financial security throughout our later years. Stay with me as we navigate this crucial area of retirement planning, where the right balance holds the key to peace of mind and true financial freedom.

Future-Proofing Your Financial Independence

When it comes to securing your financial independence in retirement, it's crucial to future-proof your strategy. The evolving landscape of economic trends, market volatility, and unforeseen life events underscores the importance of planning ahead. Future-proofing your financial independence involves assessing and mitigating potential risks while aligning your resources with your long-term goals.

Exploring income-generating opportunities beyond traditional pensions or retirement accounts can also provide added security. Moreover, a well-defined budget that anticipates healthcare costs, potential long-term care needs, and other unexpected expenses is essential for safeguarding your financial independence. This entails conducting thorough research on healthcare options, understanding insurance coverage, and making prudent decisions regarding your savings and investments. Furthermore, embracing a proactive approach to monitoring and adjusting your plan as needed is imperative. Regularly reassess your financial standing, review your asset allocation, and stay informed about legislative changes that may impact your retirement strategy. Remaining agile and adaptable allows you to navigate unforeseen challenges while maintaining confidence in your financial future. Future-proofing your financial independence isn't just about safeguarding your wealth; it's also about preserving peace of mind and the ability to enjoy the lifestyle you've envisioned. By implementing these proactive measures and continuously refining your approach, you can fortify your financial independence and embrace the next chapter of your life with confidence.

Why Insurance Isn't Just for When Times Get Rough

Insurance is often misunderstood as a safety net reserved for dire times, such as accidents, illnesses, or natural disasters. While it certainly does provide crucial support during these tough moments, its significance goes beyond just mitigating catastrophic events. In fact, insurance plays a pivotal role in maintaining financial stability and security in the long run. By recognizing this misconception, we can appreciate how insurance serves as an integral component of steady financial planning. It's not just about preparing for worst-case scenarios; rather, it's about safeguarding one's assets, health, and peace of mind in all circumstances. Whether it's protection for your health, property, or even investment portfolios, insurance can provide a layer of reassurance that enables individuals to navigate their lives with confidence and resilience. Furthermore, acknowledging the broader scope of insurance dispels the notion that it's an unnecessary expense or only pertinent when disaster strikes. Instead, it becomes apparent that insurance is a proactive tool for preserving financial well-being, ensuring that unexpected challenges or expenses don't derail long-term plans. Ultimately, embracing insurance as a fundamental part of financial planning empowers individuals to approach their futures with a sense of security and stability, irrespective of the uncertainties that may lie ahead.

Decoding the Different Flavors of Insurance: From Health to Home

Though insurance might not be the most riveting topic, understanding its role in retirement can significantly impact your financial peace of mind. When you hear the word 'insurance,' what comes to mind? Is it just health insurance and car insurance? Well, hold on tight because we're about to dive into a world where insurance takes on various forms tailored to protect your golden years. Let's start with health insurance. As you transition into retirement, healthcare becomes an even more critical consideration. Medicare typically covers Americans 65 and older, but understanding the gaps in coverage and exploring supplemental insurance options can make a world of difference. Long-term care insurance is another vital piece of the puzzle. It addresses the potential need for assistance with daily living activities as you age. Moving on to home insurance, securing your property becomes increasingly important in retirement. We'll explore different aspects of home insurance, from protection against natural disasters to liability coverage in case of accidents on your property. Then there's life insurance, a tool often associated with providing for dependents after death. However, did you know that life insurance can also be used as a powerful estate planning and wealth transfer tool? We'll decode the nuances of how life insurance fits into your overall retirement plan. And let's not forget about annuities, a form of retirement income insurance. Annuities offer a stream of payments, either for a set period or a lifetime, providing an additional layer of security in retirement. The diverse landscape of insurance options can seem overwhelming, but by decoding and understanding the different flavors of insurance, you can make informed decisions that will safeguard your retirement lifestyle.

Making Smart Choices: How to Pick the Right Insurance for Your Golden Years

Choosing the right insurance for your retirement years can be a daunting task, but with the proper guidance and understanding, it doesn't have to be a headache. When it comes to securing your financial future, making smart insurance choices is crucial. Let's delve into the key factors to consider when selecting insurance that will provide you with peace of mind and security in your golden years. First and foremost, evaluate your specific needs. Consider your health condition, family history, and lifestyle to determine the type of medical insurance that best suits your requirements. For instance, if you have pre-existing health conditions, you may require a more comprehensive health insurance plan. Next, assess your assets and liabilities. This will help you determine the coverage needed for insurances such as homeowners, auto, and liability insurance. It's essential to strike a balance between protecting your assets and ensuring your premiums are manageable. Research and compare different insurance providers. Don't settle for the first option you come across; shop around and gather quotes from various companies to ensure you're getting the best value for money. Look beyond the cost and also consider factors such as customer service, claim settlement track record, and the provider's financial strength. Understand the terms and conditions of the policies offered. Insurance jargon can be intimidating, but take the time to understand the fine print. Pay close attention to coverage limits, deductibles, copayments, exclusions, and renewal terms. You want to be well-informed about what you are purchasing. Seek professional advice if needed. If navigating the insurance landscape feels overwhelming, consider enlisting the expertise of a reputable financial advisor or insurance broker. They can provide personalized recommendations based on your unique circumstances and guide you through the decision-making process. Lastly, reassess your insurance needs periodically. Factors such as life events, economic changes, and evolving healthcare needs can affect your insurance requirements. It's important to revisit and revise your coverage as necessary to ensure it continues to align with your retirement goals. By following these guidelines, you can confidently navigate the complex world of insurance and make informed decisions that safeguard your financial well-being during your golden years.

Healthcare Considerations Beyond Medicare

Healthcare considerations are a vital component of long-term retirement planning, especially considering the potential challenges and costs associated with medical care as individuals age. Beyond Medicare, retirees need to contemplate various aspects of healthcare to ensure comprehensive coverage as they transition into their senior years. One key consideration is long-term care insurance, which provides coverage for services not typically covered by health insurance, Medicare, or Medicaid. Long-term care insurance can help offset expenses related to assisted living, nursing homes, in-home care, and other long-term care needs. There are annuities that offer long-term care type benefits (well-being riders) that you don't have to prequalify for. Finding the right one for you requires a retirement strategist who specializes in annuities. Another crucial aspect is understanding the different supplemental insurance options available, such as Medigap policies, which can cover co-payments, deductibles, and other out-of-pocket costs that Medicare may not fully address. Retirees should also assess their potential need for additional prescription drug coverage, either through a Medicare Part D plan or a Medicare Advantage plan that includes prescription drug coverage. Moreover, it's essential to explore the evolving landscape of telemedicine and digital health resources, which can provide convenient access to healthcare professionals and specialists, particularly for retirees living in remote areas. Considering the impact of technology on healthcare, staying informed about digital health tools and advancements can empower retirees to manage their wellness effectively. Furthermore, pre-retirees should also investigate the potential benefits of health savings accounts (HSAs) as part of their retirement planning strategy. HSAs offer tax advantages and can be used to cover qualified medical expenses, providing a valuable financial cushion for healthcare costs in retirement. Lastly, adopting a proactive approach to healthy living and preventative care plays a significant role in managing healthcare expenses in retirement. By embracing lifestyle choices that promote wellness and prevent chronic diseases, retirees can potentially reduce their long-term healthcare costs and enhance their overall quality of life. With these considerations in mind, addressing healthcare beyond Medicare is pivotal in crafting a comprehensive retirement plan that prioritizes physical well-being and financial security.

Estate Planning Considerations for Retirees

When it comes to estate planning, retirees have unique considerations to keep in mind to ensure their assets are protected, and their loved ones are taken care of. As you transition into retirement, reviewing and updating your estate plan to reflect your current financial situation and goals is important.

One essential aspect of estate planning for retirees is creating a comprehensive will. A will outlines how you want your assets to be distributed after your passing, ensuring that your wishes are carried out. Be sure to carefully consider who you want to inherit your assets and any specific bequests you wish to make. In addition to a will, retirees may also want to consider establishing trusts as part of their estate plan. Trusts can offer more flexibility and control over how your assets are distributed, allowing you to provide for your loved ones in a structured way. There are various types of trusts to consider, such as revocable living trusts, irrevocable trusts, and charitable trusts, each serving different purposes and offering unique benefits.

Working with a knowledgeable estate planning attorney can help you determine which type of trust aligns best with your goals. Trusts can also help minimize estate taxes and avoid the probate process, making it easier for your beneficiaries to access their inheritance. By placing assets in a trust, you can ensure that they are managed according to your wishes and provide for future generations in a tax-efficient manner. Another important consideration for retirees is planning for incapacity. As you age, there may come a time when you can no longer make decisions for yourself. By appointing a durable power of attorney and healthcare proxy, you can designate someone you trust to make important financial and medical decisions on your behalf if you become incapacitated. It's essential to choose individuals who are reliable and capable of acting in your best interests.

Retirees should consider creating an advance directive or living will to outline their wishes regarding end-of-life medical care. This document can provide guidance to your healthcare proxy and medical professionals in the event that you are unable to communicate your preferences. Finally, don't forget about beneficiary designations on your retirement accounts and life insurance policies. These assets typically pass directly to your named beneficiaries outside of the probate process, so it's crucial to keep these designations up to date to ensure your assets go to the right people.

Reviewing and updating your beneficiary designations regularly can help avoid unintended consequences and ensure that your assets are distributed according to your wishes. Estate planning can be a complex and personal process, especially for retirees with accumulated assets and a desire to provide for their loved ones. By taking the time to create a thoughtful estate plan that addresses your unique needs and goals, you can achieve peace of mind knowing that your legacy will be preserved and your loved ones will be cared for. Consult with a qualified estate planning attorney to guide you through the process and ensure that your estate plan reflects your intentions and supports your financial legacy. Remember, estate planning is a continuous journey, so make it a priority to regularly review and update your plan as your circumstances evolve.

Dodging Financial Curveballs: Smart Moves for Tough Times

Retirement planning is like a game of chess, with each move paving the way for your future financial well-being. But just as in life, where unexpected challenges arise, economic realities can throw curveballs that disrupt even the best-laid retirement plans. In this section, we delve into the strategies and smart moves you can employ to navigate through tough times and emerge with your retirement intact.

1. Emergency Fund Essentials: The foundation of any sound financial plan, the emergency fund provides a safety net when unexpected expenses crop up. With enough cash reserves to cover 3-6 months' worth of living expenses, you can sidestep the impact of sudden medical bills or car repairs without jeopardizing your long-term financial security. We'll explore how to build and maintain this crucial cushion, offering practical tips to make it a reality for everyone.

2. Flexibility in Retirement Income: When economic downturns hit, traditional sources of retirement income may experience fluctuations. Adaptability is key, and considering alternative income streams beyond pensions and savings can buffer any financial shocks. From part-

time work to rental income, we'll guide you through the options available to supplement your retirement funds and provide added stability when market conditions get rocky.

3. Rigorous Expense Management: As retirees, keeping a close eye on expenses is crucial. Smart budgeting and trimming unnecessary costs can free up funds during lean periods and help preserve your retirement nest egg. We'll share practical advice on identifying areas where savings can be made without sacrificing your quality of life, empowering you to weather any financial storm with confidence.

4. Diversification Strategies: A diversified investment portfolio can serve as a shield against market volatility. By spreading your investments across different asset classes, you can mitigate risk and enhance the potential for long-term growth. We'll provide insights into crafting a well-balanced portfolio tailored to your risk tolerance and retirement goals, ensuring resilience in the face of economic uncertainty.

5. Guaranteed income Stream: It is crucial to have a guaranteed income stream in your retirement portfolio. Ensuring that you and your spouse have protected lifetime income provides peace of mind. Even if you are a risk-taker and want to maximize your earnings, it's important to consider the possibility that anything can happen to you unexpectedly. In such a situation, your

less risk-taking spouse may be left making uncomfortable financial decisions. Including an Income Annuity in your portfolio can provide guaranteed lifetime income and peace of mind.

Review and Renew: Keeping Your Retirement Plan Agile

Remember to stay flexible when planning for retirement. The financial world is always changing, so your retirement plan should change along with it. First, take a good look at your money situation, including investments, savings, and retirement accounts. Consider things like how the market is doing, inflation, and how much you'll need in the future. It's important to review your comfort level with taking risks. As you get older, you might feel differently about risk, so make sure your investments match your current feelings. Big life events like getting married, having kids, or dealing with unexpected health problems can also shake up your finances, so be ready to tweak your plan. Pay attention to any new tax rules, government benefits, or how the market is doing, and get advice if you need help. Also, make sure to check in regularly with a retirement planner for advice. Keep learning about new financial strategies and tools, so you can tweak your retirement plan as needed to keep it strong and flexible. The goal is to set yourself up for a stable and worry-free retirement.

Retirement can bring up all kinds of feelings – from excitement about the freedom to uncertainty about money. But it's important to tackle this new phase with a positive attitude and resilience. Remember, your hard work and careful planning have set you up for a fulfilling retirement. Embracing change, nurturing relationships, and staying financially savvy are key. Also, taking care of your health, staying active, and giving back can make your retirement years even more meaningful. Keep in mind that resilience is about facing challenges with determination and optimism. So, with the right mindset, strong connections, financial planning, good health, and meaningful contributions, you can build a resilient and fulfilling retirement.

A well-rounded retirement portfolio should address the three key phases of retirement: Accumulation, Distribution, and Preservation. Accumulation is the process of building and growing your savings, Distribution involves making withdrawals from your funds, and Preservation ensures you have a reliable source of lifetime income that will support you throughout retirement.